NICKY BIRD

iThink Books

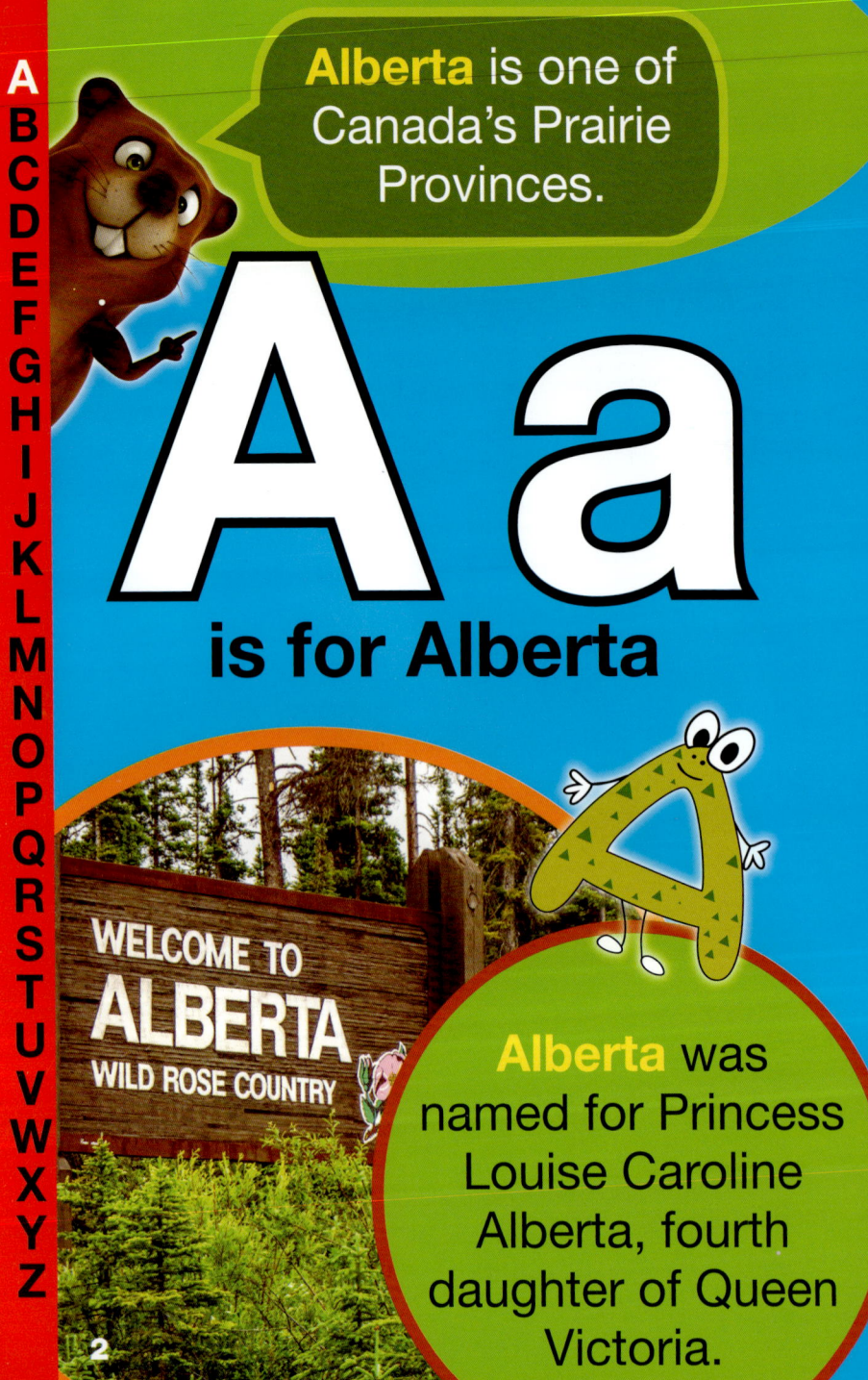

Alberta's neighbours are British Columbia to the west, Northwest Territories to the north, Saskatchewan to the east and the U.S. state of Montana to the south.

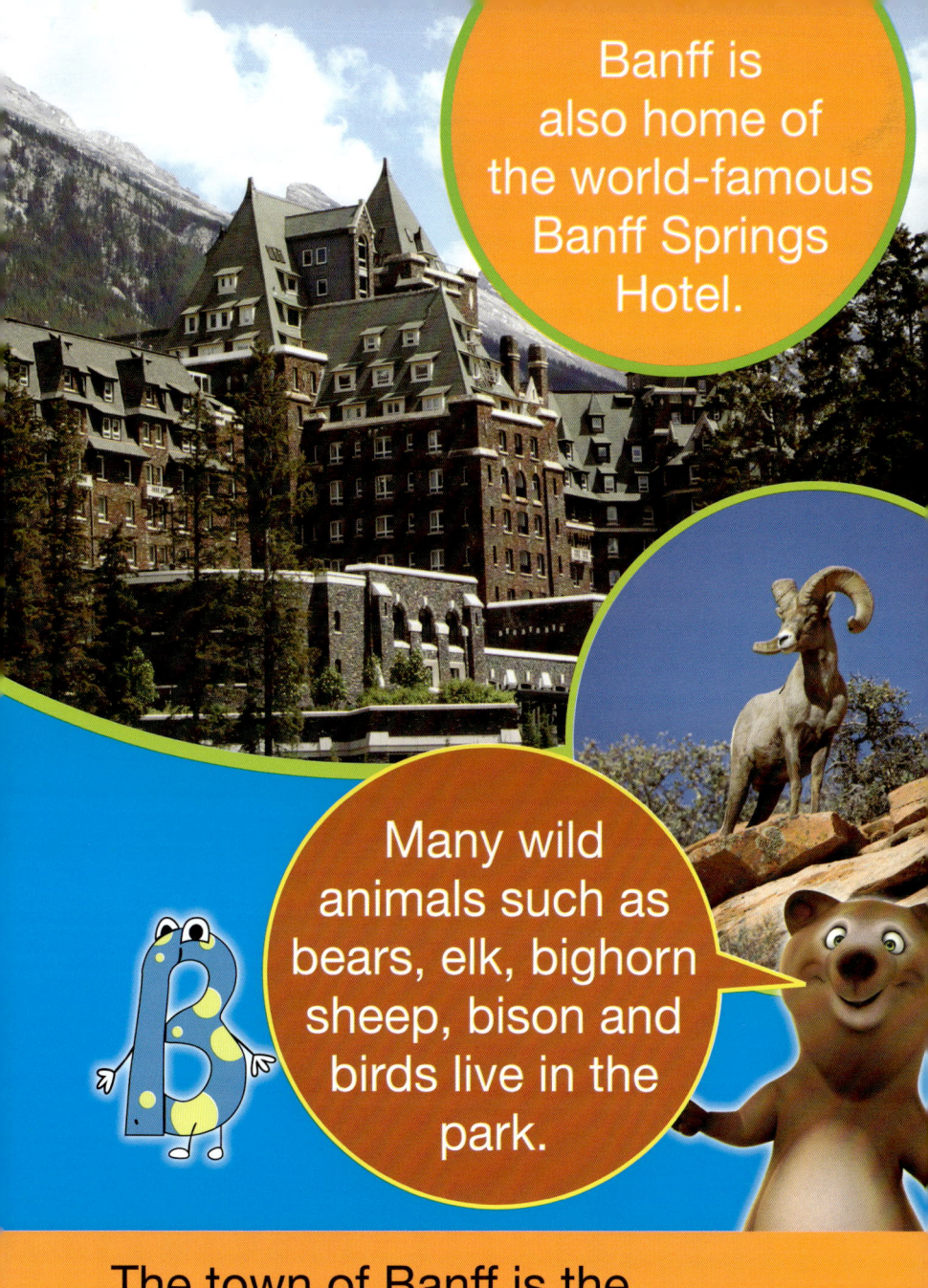

Banff is also home of the world-famous Banff Springs Hotel.

Many wild animals such as bears, elk, bighorn sheep, bison and birds live in the park.

The town of Banff is the highest town in Canada.

A B C D E F G H I J K L M N O P Q R S T U V W X Y Z

The **Calgary Stampede** is called the "Greatest Outdoor Show on Earth."

The rodeo is one of the biggest in the world.

People wear white Stetson hats at the Stampede. Their white cowboy hats are a symbol of the Stampede and of Calgary.

The midway has fun rides and shows.

Cc
is for Calgary Stampede

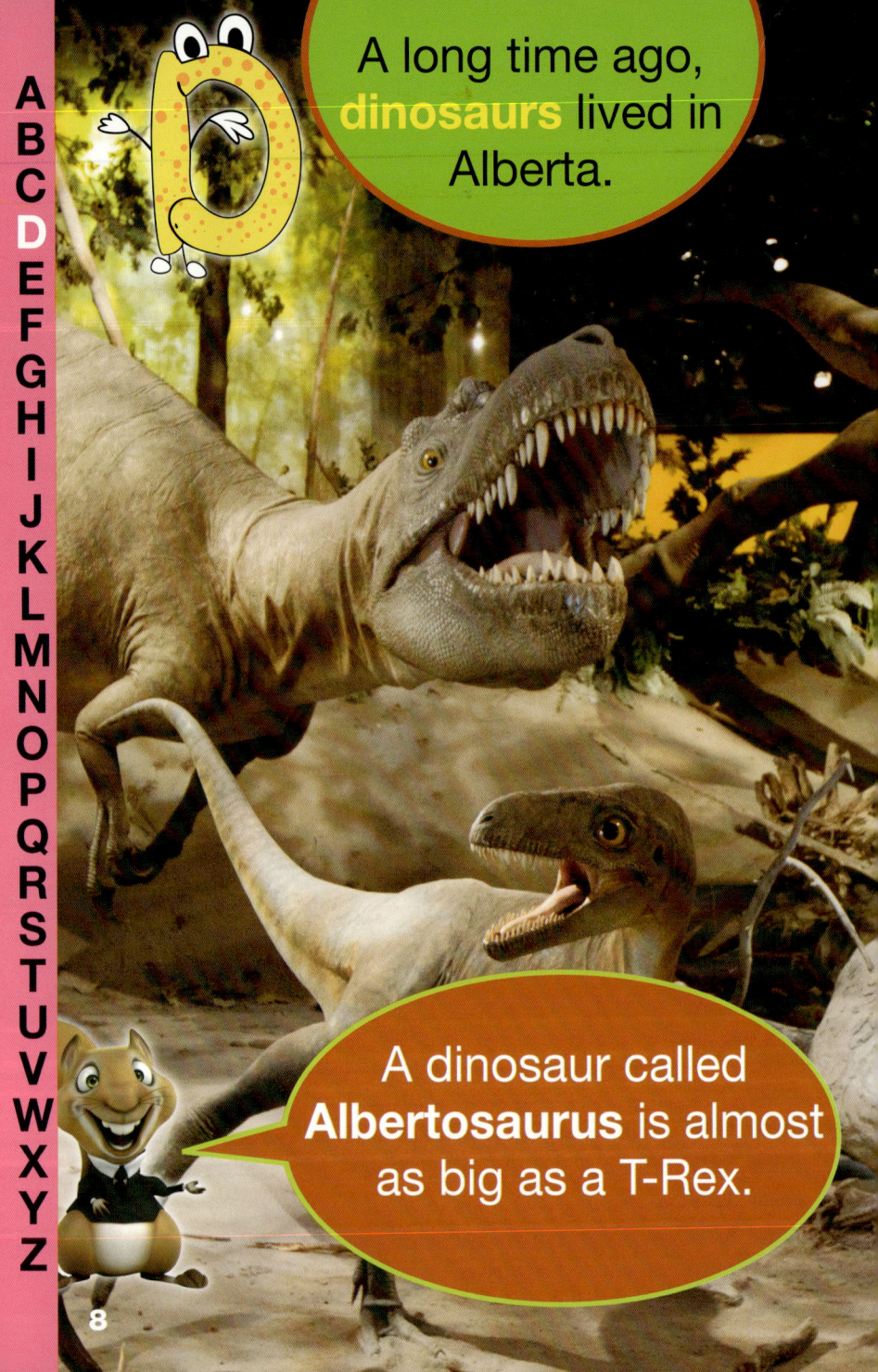

A long time ago, **dinosaurs** lived in Alberta.

A dinosaur called **Albertosaurus** is almost as big as a T-Rex.

You can see dinosaur fossils in many Alberta museums.

Dd
is for dinosaur

The Royal Tyrrell Museum in Drumheller has fossils, dinosaur bones and large models of the huge dinosaurs that lived here.

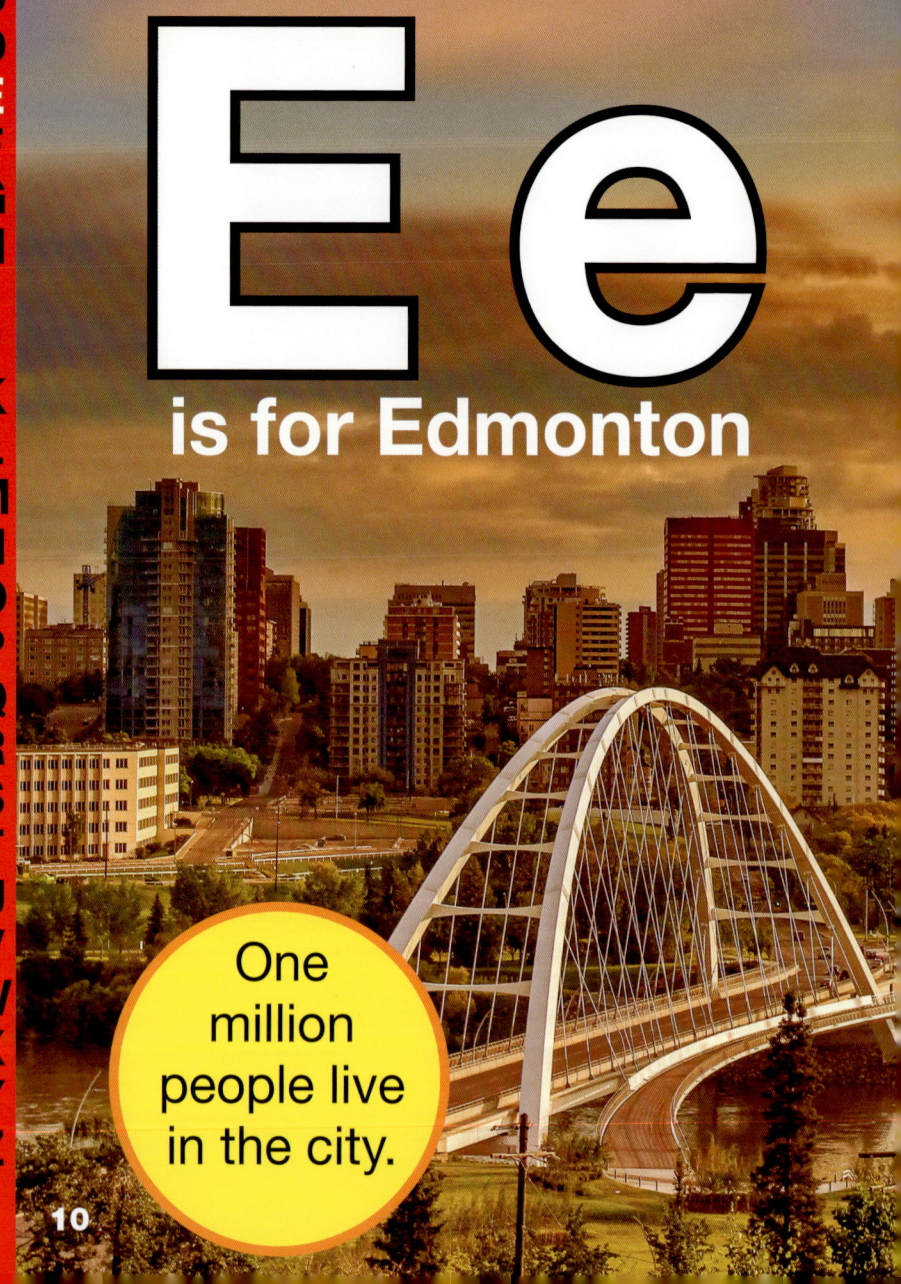

Edmonton is Alberta's capital city.

Ee
is for Edmonton

One million people live in the city.

Edmonton's river valley park is the largest urban park in North America.

Some people call Edmonton "Festival City." More than 40 festivals are held here every year.

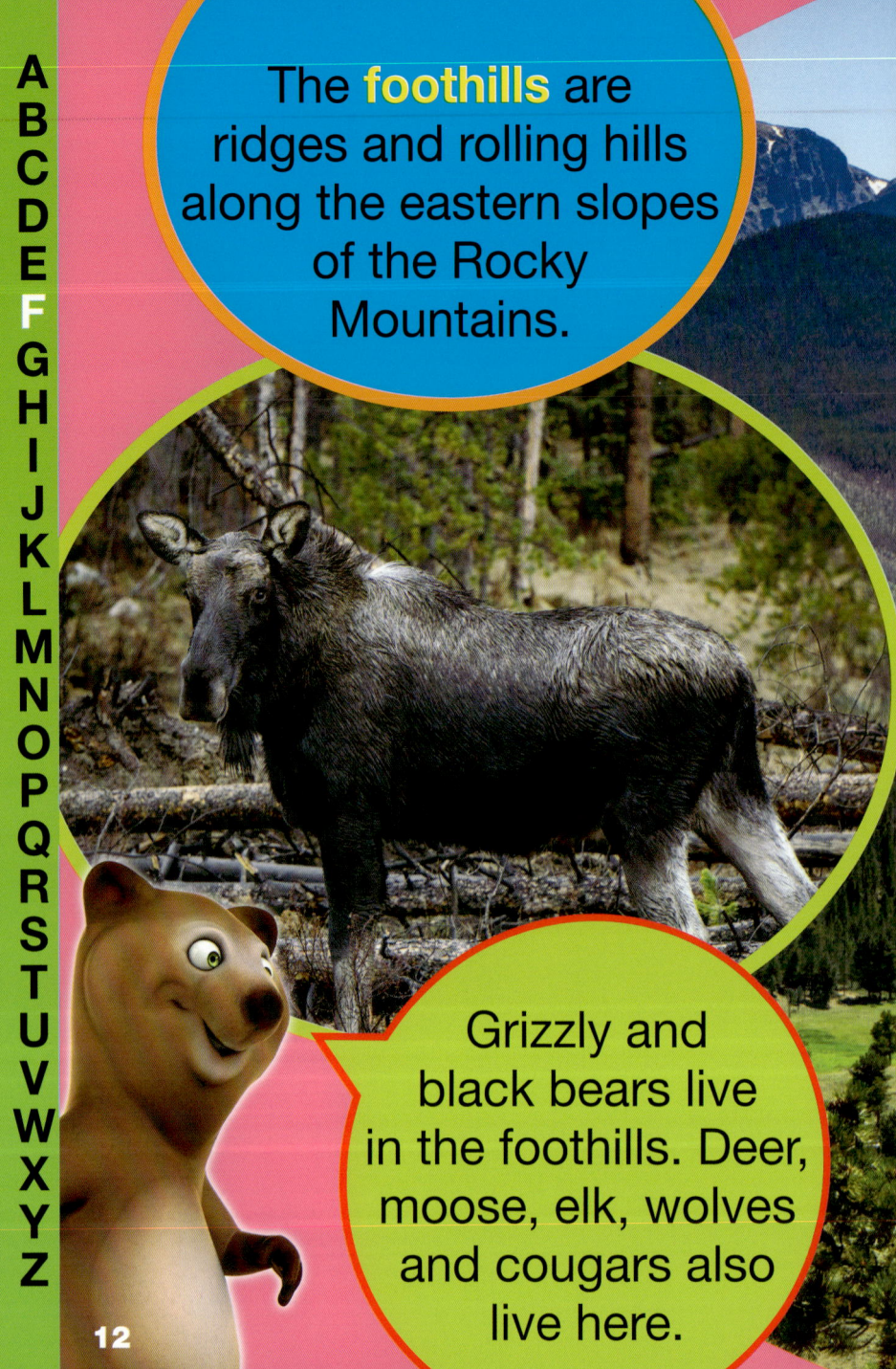

The **foothills** are ridges and rolling hills along the eastern slopes of the Rocky Mountains.

Grizzly and black bears live in the foothills. Deer, moose, elk, wolves and cougars also live here.

F f
is for foothills

Vast spruce and pine forests cover these hills. Aspens, birches and willows also grow here.

A B C D E F **G** H I J K L M N O P Q R S T U V W X Y Z

Gg

is for glaciers

Glaciers are huge sheets of thick ice. They look like snow from far away.

14

There are more than 1000 glaciers in the Rocky Mountains.

Glaciers actually move like very slow rivers. Most glaciers move only a few centimetres per day.

A B C D E F G H I J K L M N O P Q R S T U V W X Y Z

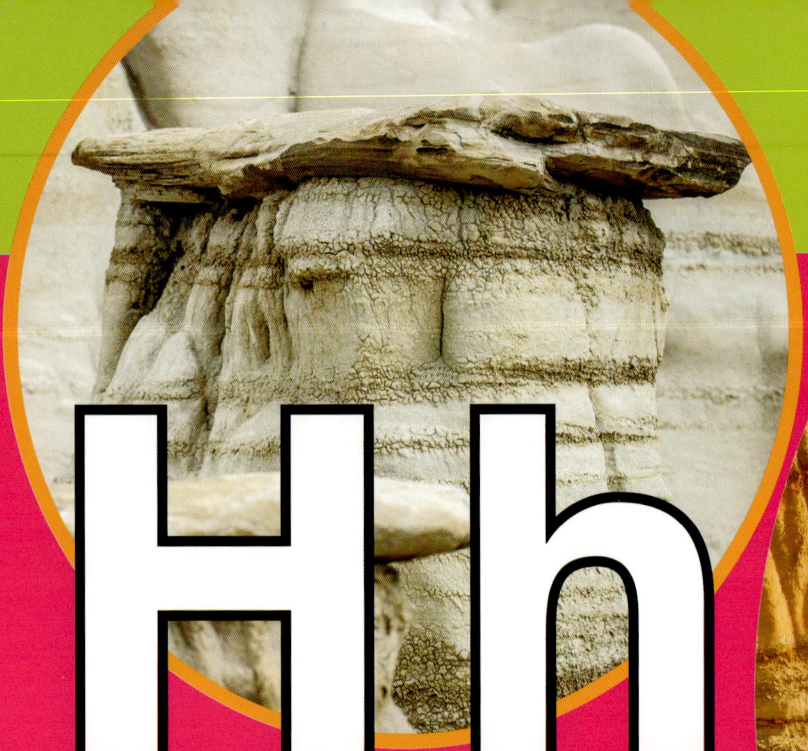

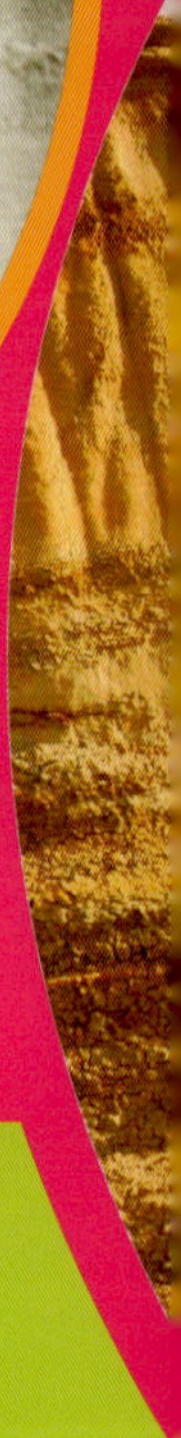

Hh

is for hoodoos

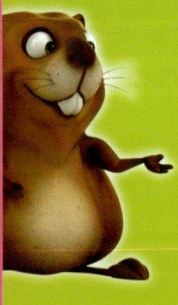

Hoodoos are made of soft rock under a "hat" of hard rock. Rain and wind wear away the soft rock. The part under the hard hat is protected and strange shapes form over hundreds of years.

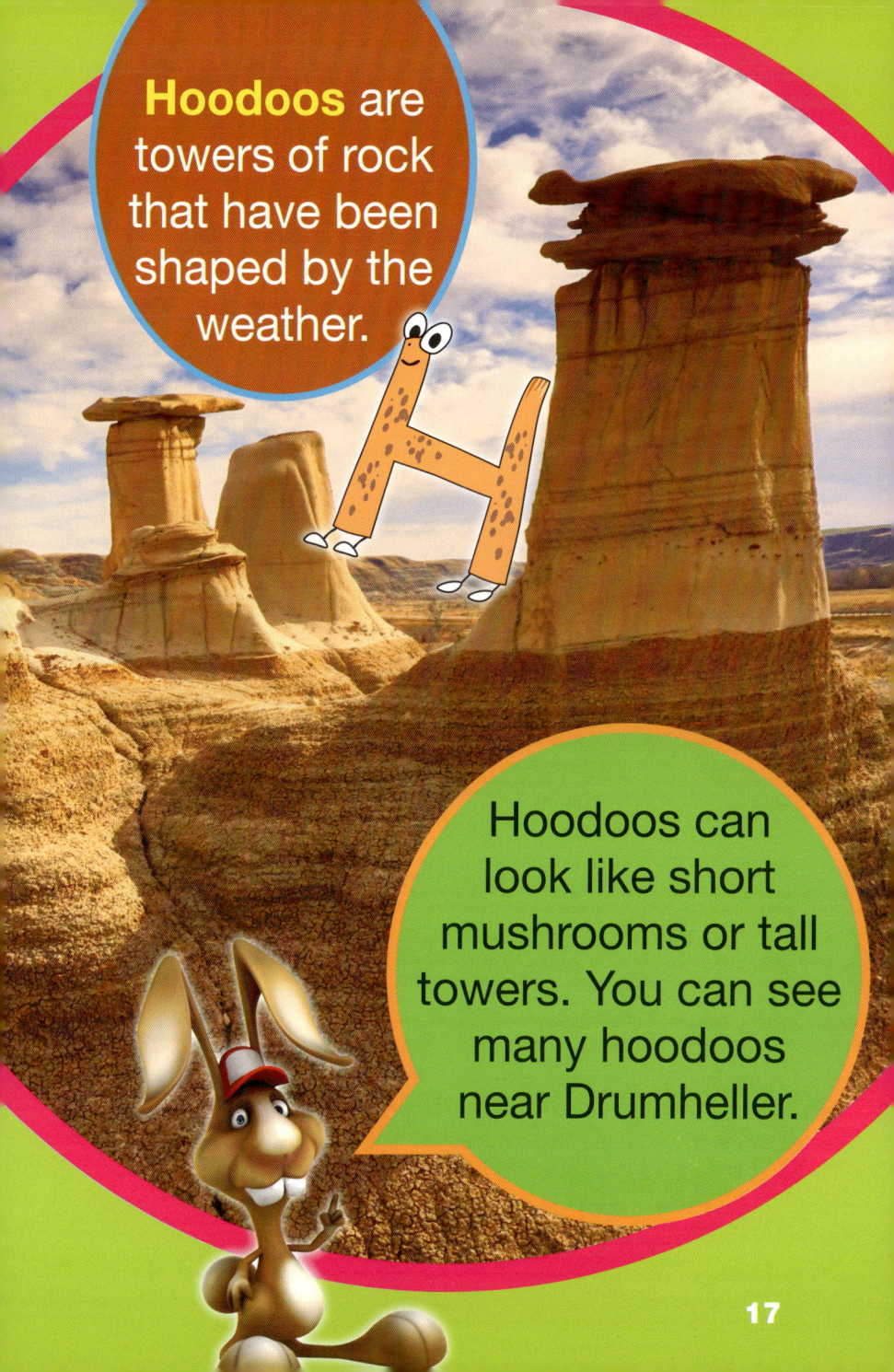

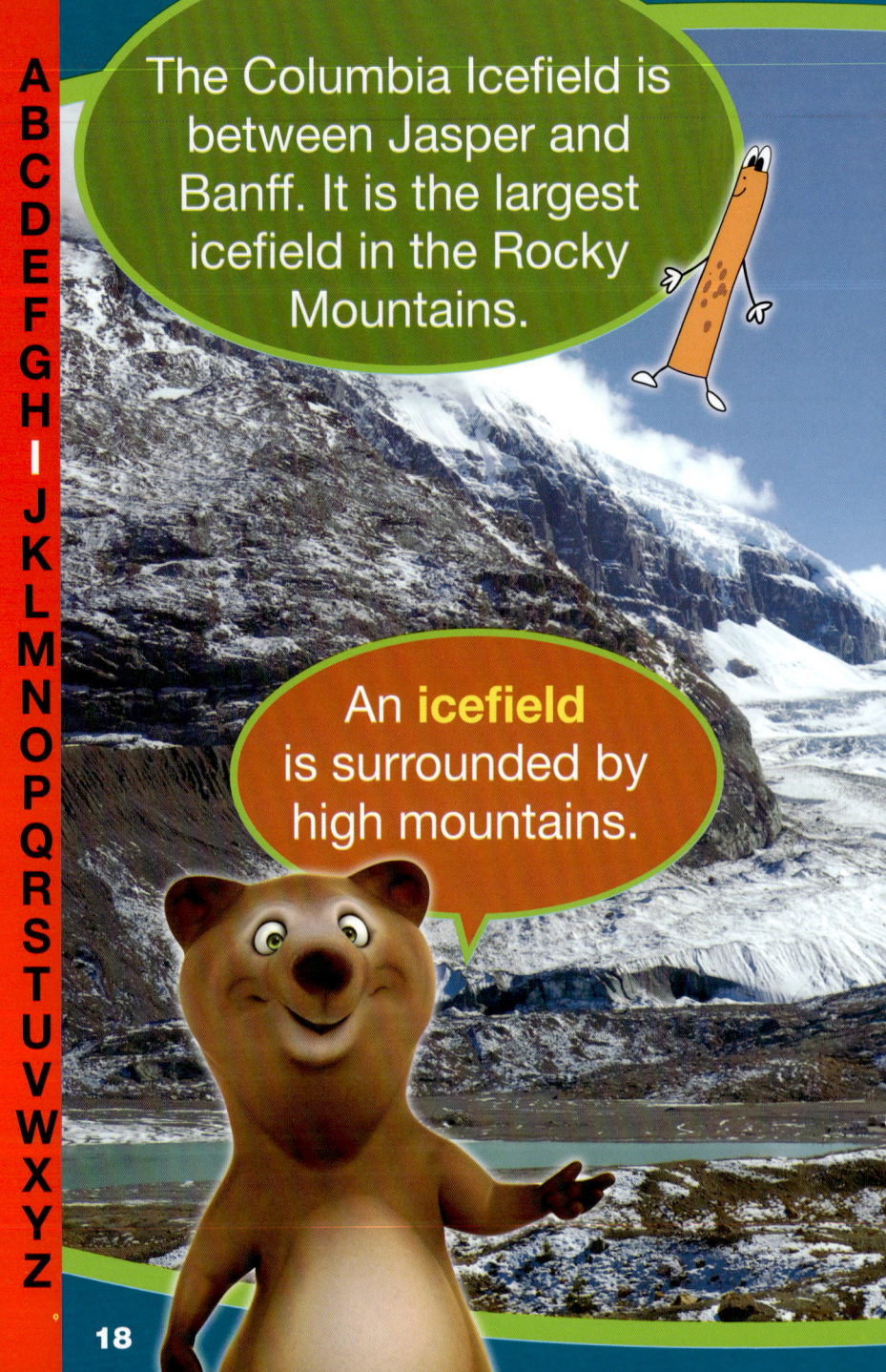

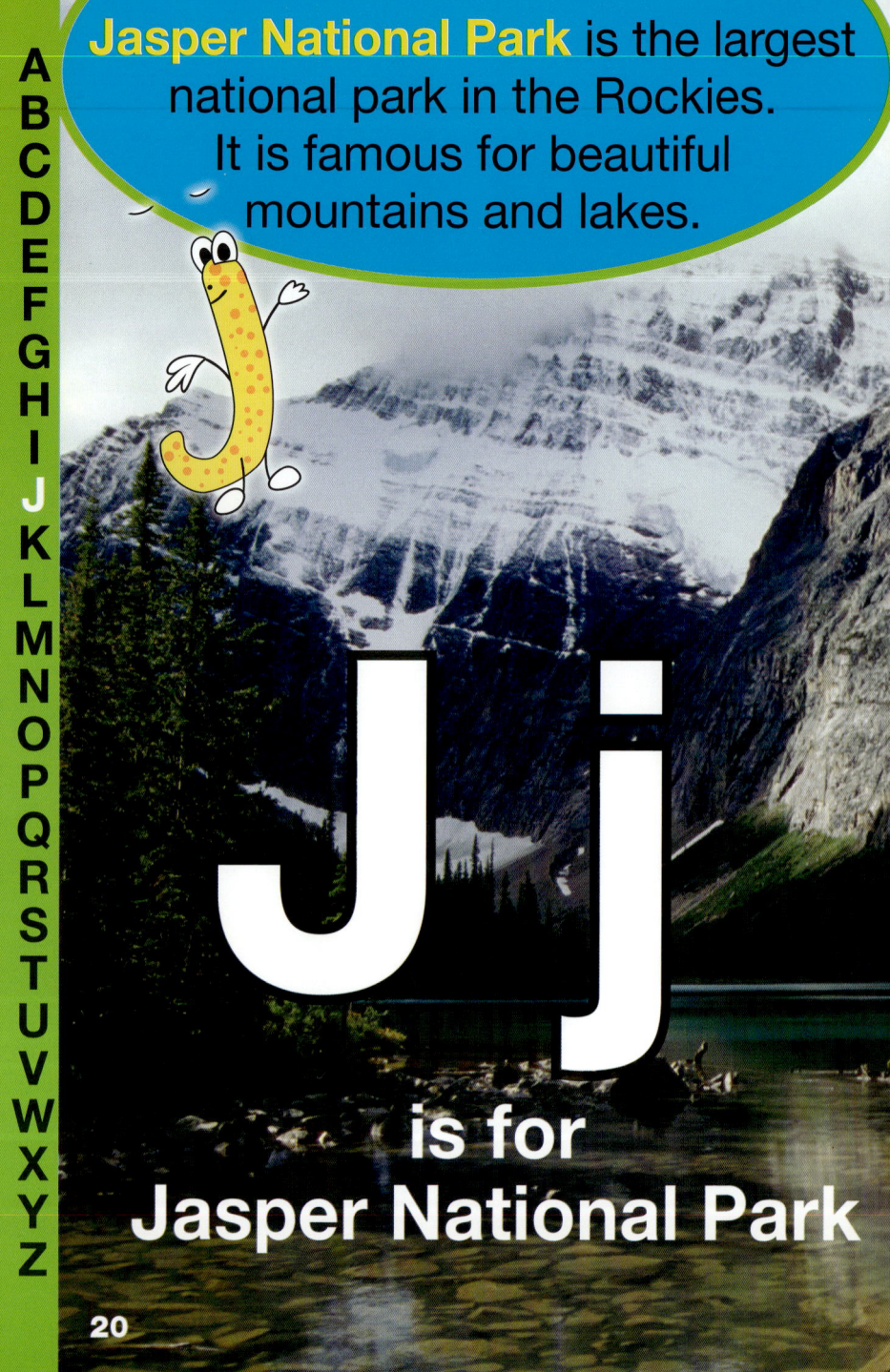

Jasper National Park is the largest national park in the Rockies. It is famous for beautiful mountains and lakes.

Jj
is for
Jasper National Park

Many wild animals such as bighorn sheep, elk, bears and marmots live in the park.

Maligne Lake is the longest lake in the Rockies.

A B C D E F G H I J **K** L M N O P Q R S T U V W X Y Z

Visitors can go hiking, fishing, mountain biking, caving (spelunking) and camping in summer, and alpine and nordic skiing in winter.

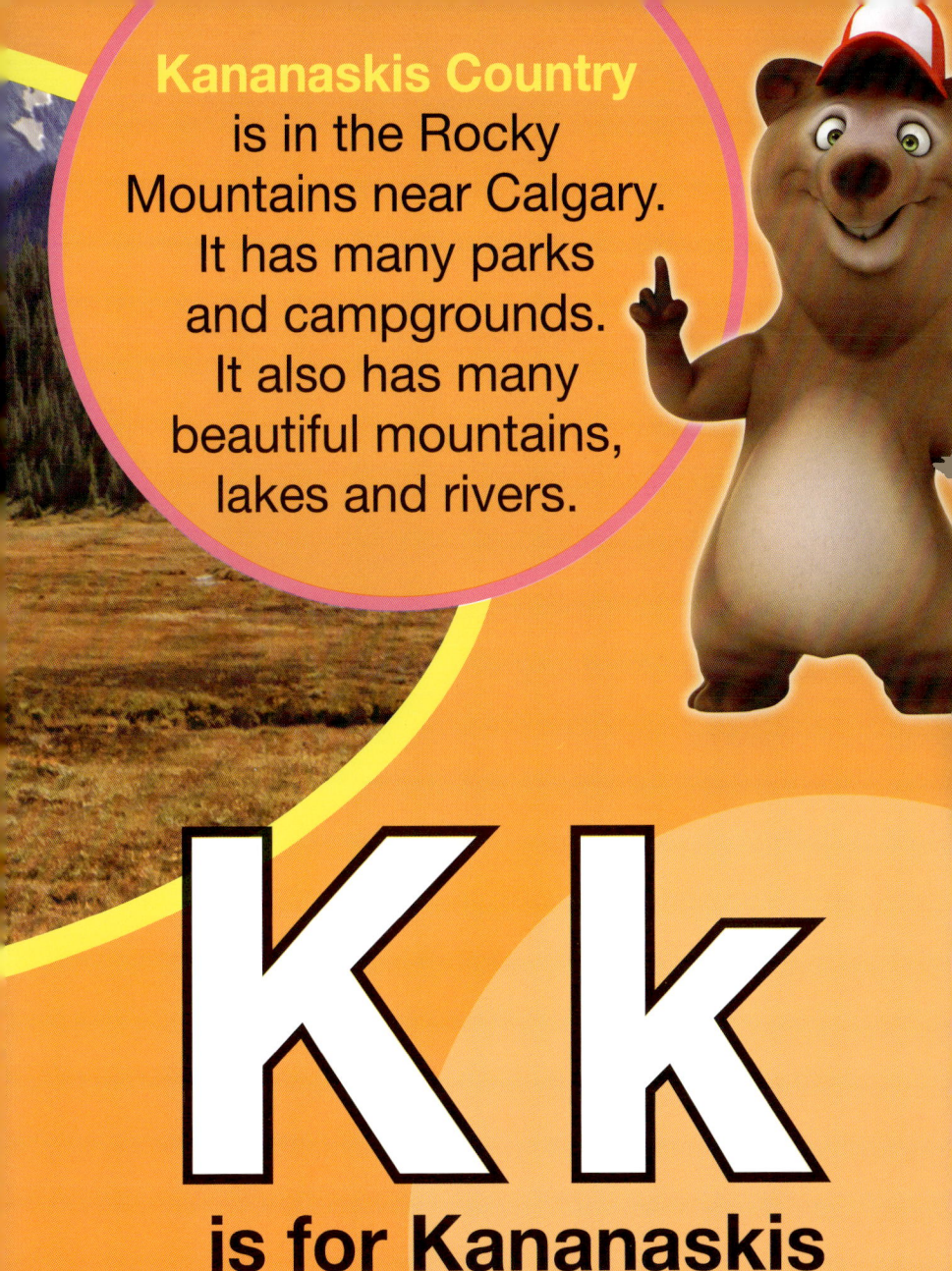

Kananaskis Country is in the Rocky Mountains near Calgary. It has many parks and campgrounds. It also has many beautiful mountains, lakes and rivers.

Kk

is for Kananaskis Country

Lake Louise is near Banff in the Rockies. The water of the lake is a beautiful greenish blue colour.

Ll

is for Lake Louise

People come from all over the world just to visit this beautiful lake.

You can hike around the lake or go canoeing and kayaking. In winter, people skate on the lake.

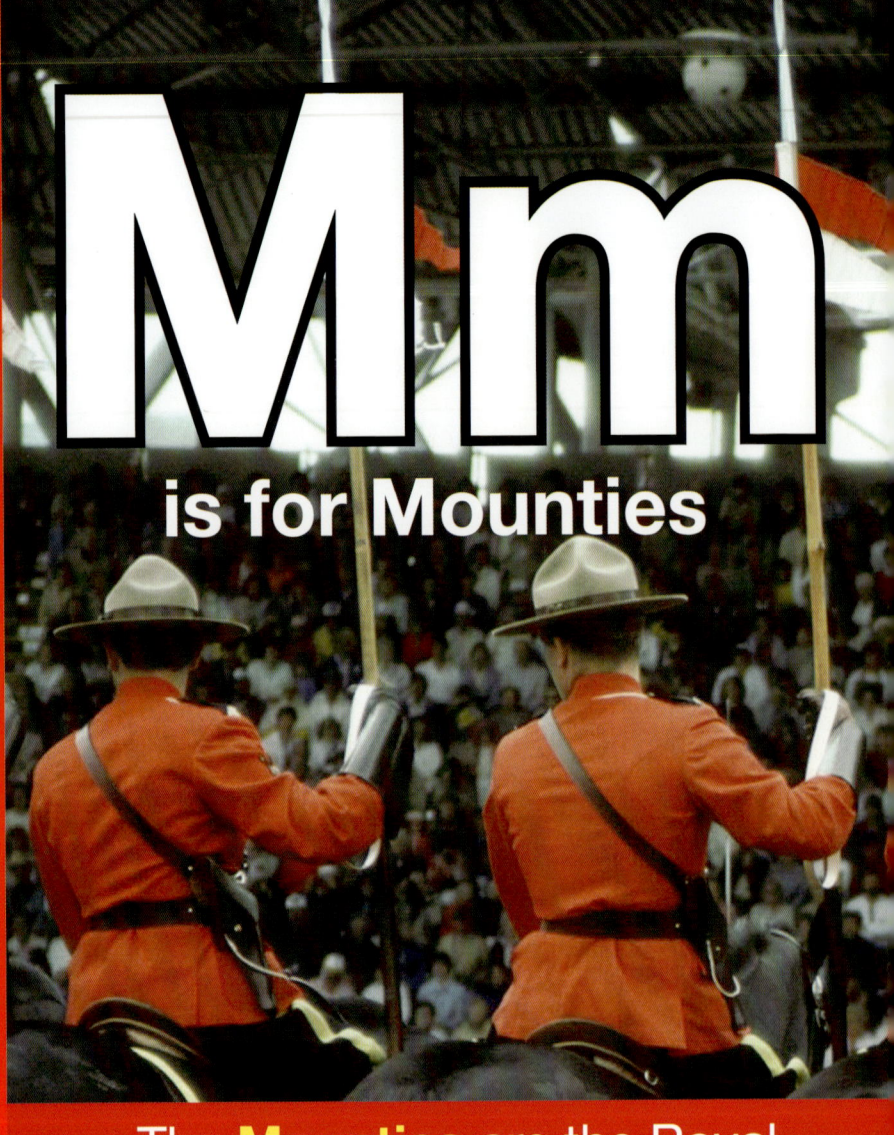

Mm
is for Mounties

The **Mounties** are the Royal Canadian Mounted Police (RCMP). They are famous for their red serge coats and wide-brimmed hats.

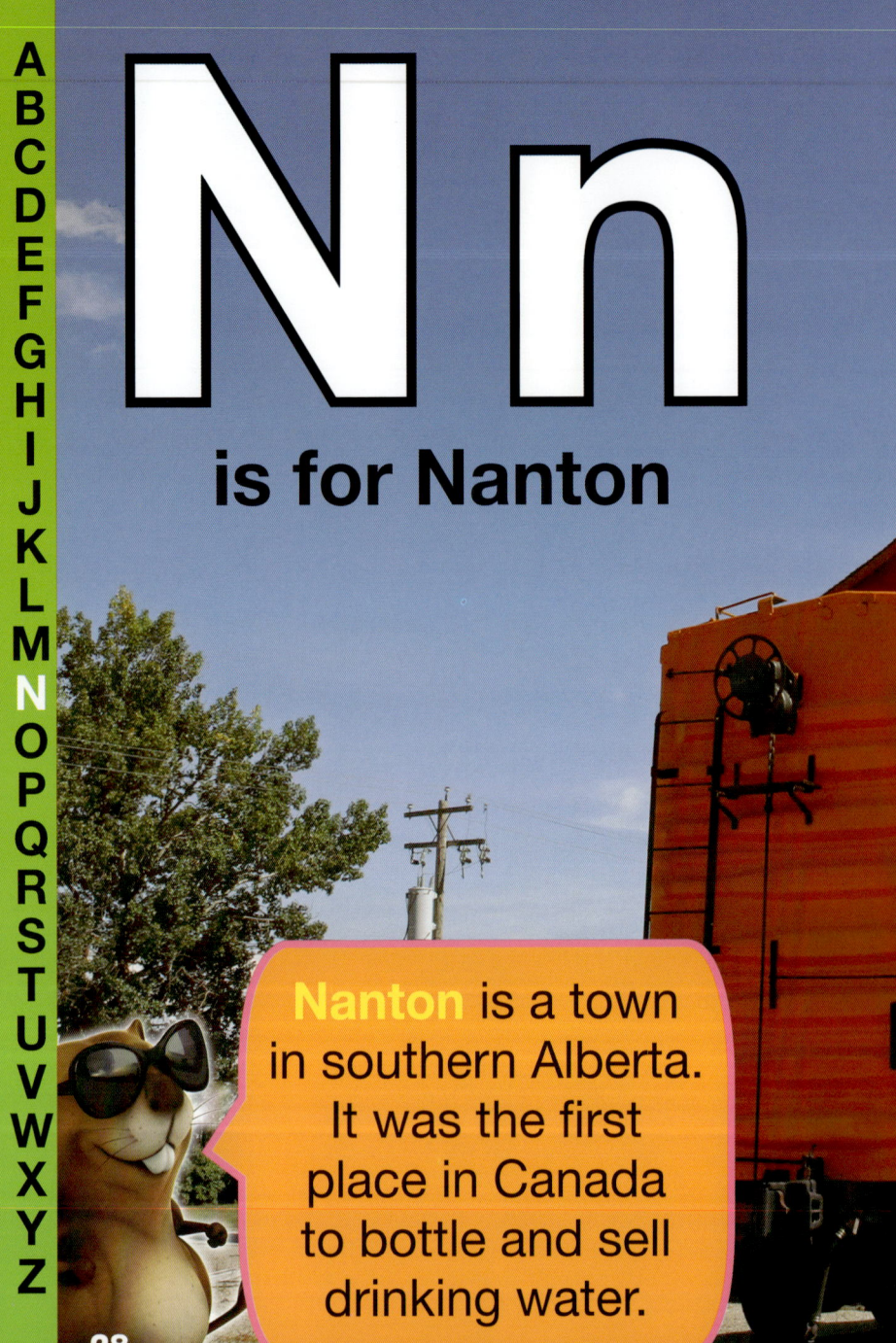

Some places to visit in Nanton are:
- one of the few remaining original grain elevators,
- an aviation museum and
- the many antique shops.

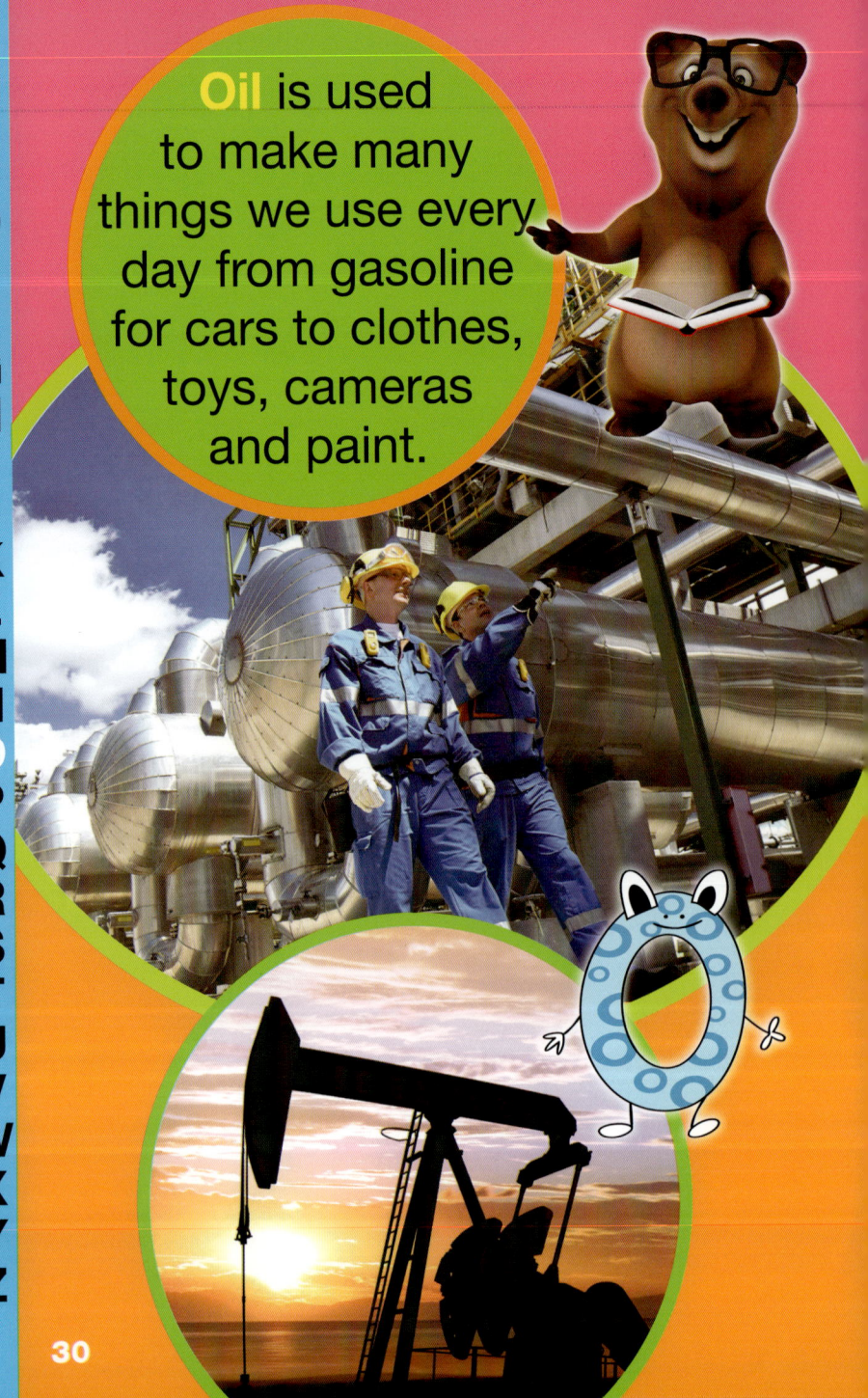

Oil is used to make many things we use every day from gasoline for cars to clothes, toys, cameras and paint.

Oil is an important natural resource in Alberta.

Oo is for oil

The first oil well was drilled in Turner Valley in 1914. Alberta also gets oil from the oil sands near Fort McMurray.

Pp
is for petroglyphs

Petroglyph means "stone writing." A long time ago, people carved pictures into rocks. The pictures tell a story.

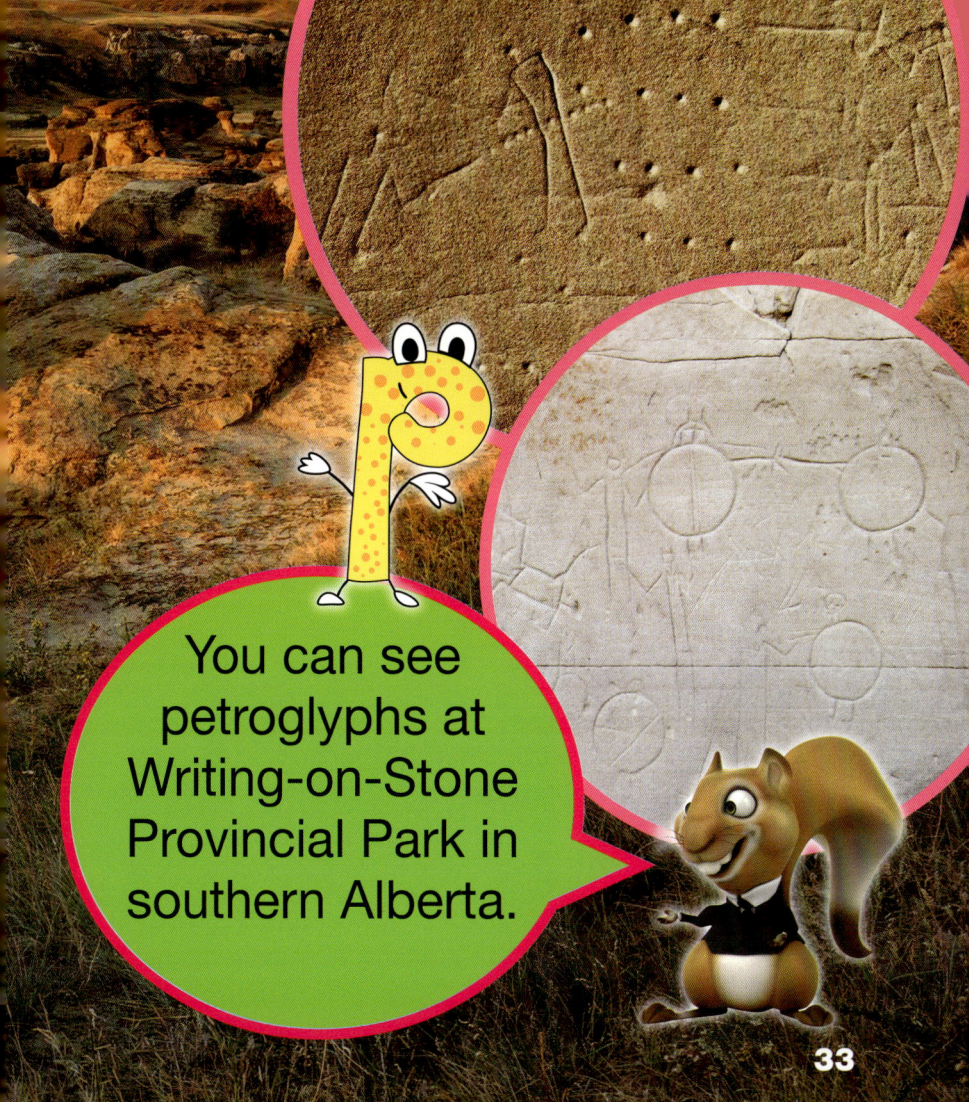

You can see petroglyphs at Writing-on-Stone Provincial Park in southern Alberta.

ABCDEFGHIJKLMNOPQRSTUVWXYZ

Indigenous peoples use porcupine quills to decorate their clothing and other objects.

Qq

is for quillwork

They made dyes from plants, and they dyed the quills many bright colours.

A B C D E F G H I J K L M N O P Q R S T U V W X Y Z

Rr
is for Rocky Mountains

The **Rocky Mountains** were formed millions of years ago. These high mountains stretch from northern British Columbia through Alberta and then into the United States all the way to New Mexico.

Mount Columbia is the highest mountain in Alberta at 3747 metres. That's almost 4 kilometres high!

Mount Robson in British Columbia is the highest mountain in the Canadian Rockies at 3954 metres.

Saskatoons grow on bushes in the woods and on hillsides. The berries ripen in July.

They were an important food for Indigenous peoples.

S s

is for Saskatoon berries

Saskatoons look a little like blueberries, but they taste very different.

T t

is for tipi

A *tipi* is a cone-shaped tent. It was used by Indigenous people who lived on the prairies. These people moved from place to place. They were called nomads.

Tipis were made from wooden poles covered with buffalo skins.

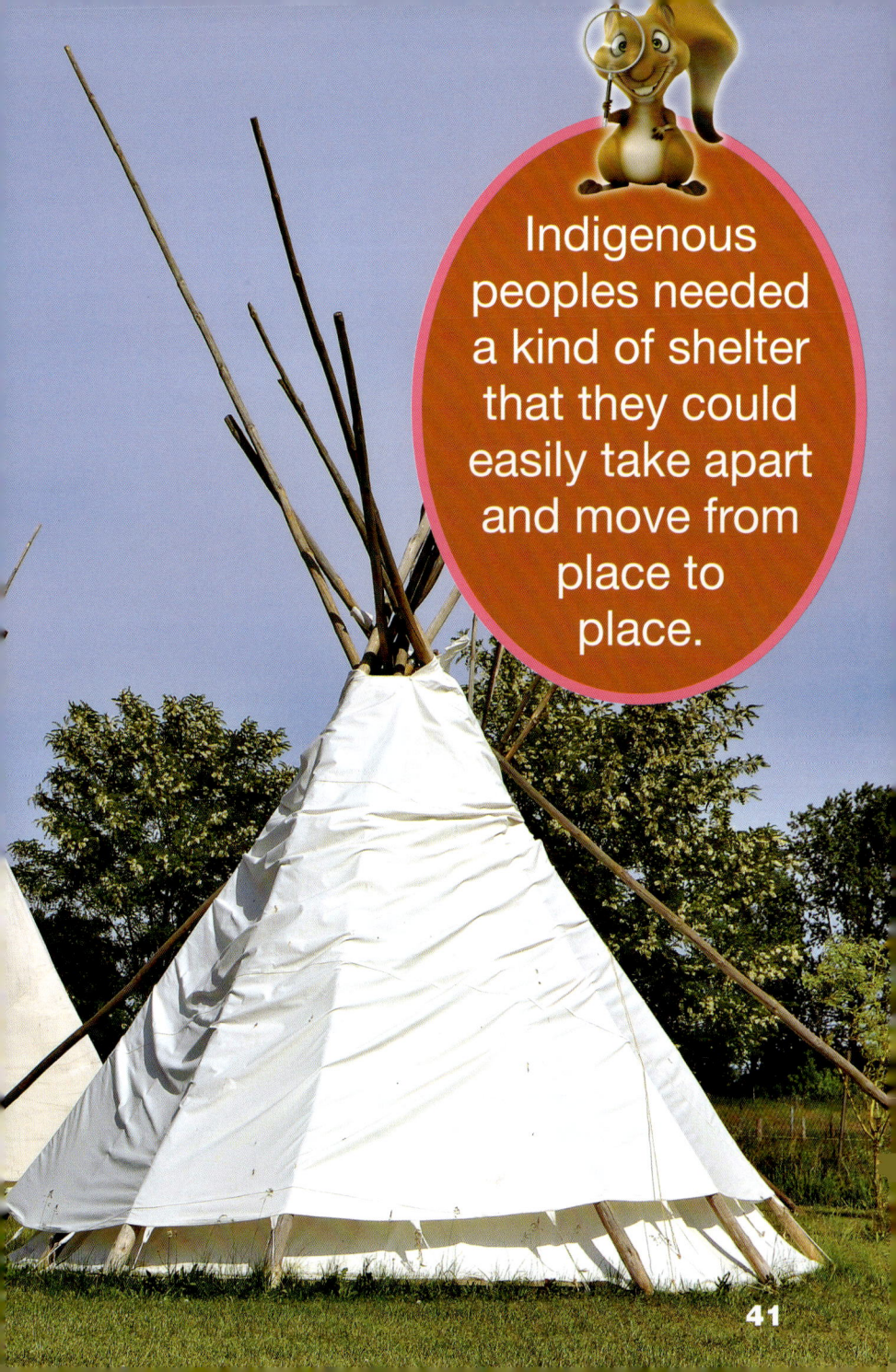

Indigenous peoples needed a kind of shelter that they could easily take apart and move from place to place.

Many of the people that came to Alberta to farm came from Ukraine, a country in Europe. Almost 200,000 **Ukrainians** came to Canada. Many came to be farmers in Alberta.

They brought their culture, customs and food with them like Easter eggs, pyrogies, Ukrainian dancing and so much more.

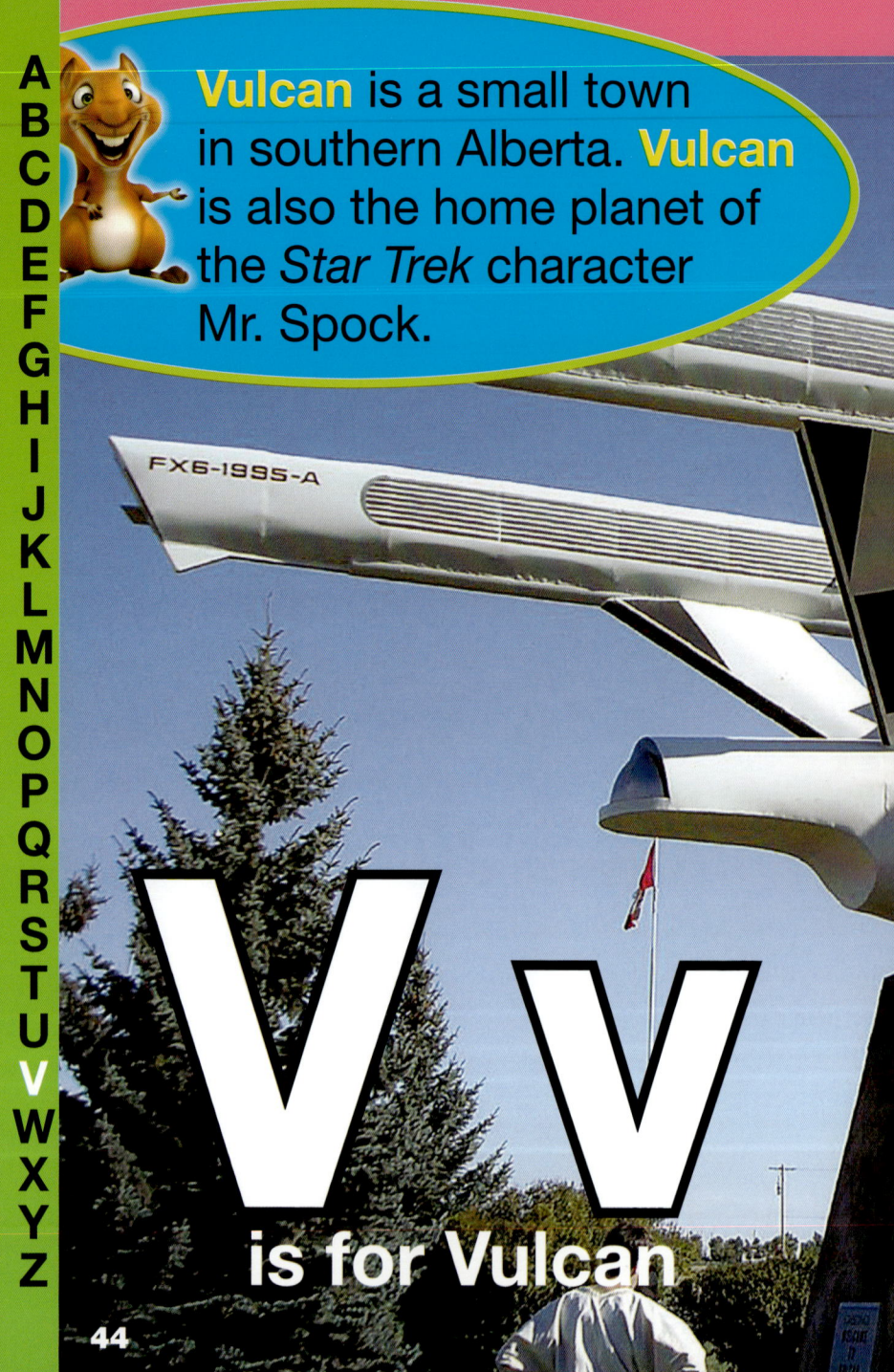

A B C D E F G H I J K L M N O P Q R S T U V W X Y Z

Vulcan is a small town in southern Alberta. **Vulcan** is also the home planet of the *Star Trek* character Mr. Spock.

Vv
is for Vulcan

The town wanted more visitors to come. They built a *Star Trek*–themed Tourism and Trek Station.

Beside the station is a model of the starship *Enterprise*. There is also a bust of Spock, a Transporter and a mural of all the *Star Trek* doctors.

These bright pink flowers grow on small shrubs. **Wild roses** bloom from May to August.

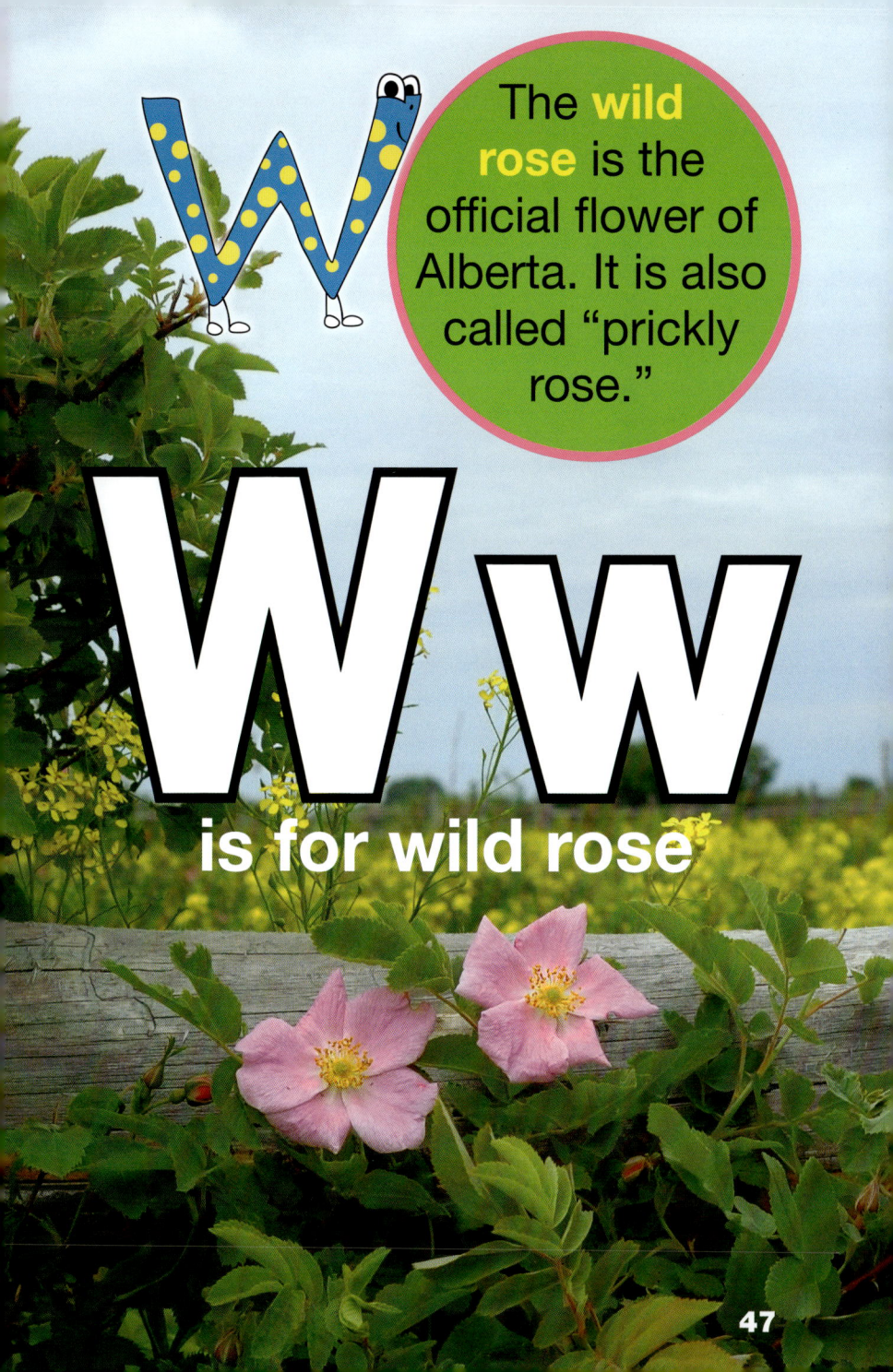

The **wild rose** is the official flower of Alberta. It is also called "prickly rose."

Ww is for wild rose

Xx
is for X-country skiing

Cross-country skiing is a popular winter sport in Alberta.

It is a way of travelling across the snow, using long, skinny skis and poles. Wax on the bottom of the skis helps them grip the snow.

People from Norway, Sweden and Finland brought the sport to Canada in the 1850s.

Becky Scott from Vegreville won a gold medal in cross-country skiing at the 2002 Olympics.

Yy
is for Yamnuska

Yamnuska is the Indigenous name for a mountain in the Rockies close to the town of Canmore.

Its name means "wall of stone" in the Stoney Nakoda language.

Yamnuska is a popular destination for hikers and climbers.

A B C D E F G H I J K L M N O P Q R S T U V W X Y Z

Edmonton and Calgary each have a zoo. You can visit a **zoo** to see wild animals from all around the world.

Z z
is for zoo

Zoos have special programs to teach people about the animals. You can learn about animal behaviour, what the animals eat and how they live.

Zoos do a lot of work to help protect animals that live in the wild.

Games and Puzzles

Deer are very common across Alberta.
Can you **find 10 differences** between these two pictures?

There are many great ski resorts in Alberta's Rocky Mountains. Can you **help the lost skier** find the snowboarder?

Games and Puzzles

Connect the dots to reveal the newest exhibit at the Royal Tyrrell Museum!

All kinds of animals live in Jasper National Park. Can you **find 10 differences** between these two pictures.

Games and Puzzles

Help this hiker follow the path to Mount Robson!

Game and puzzle answers.

p. 54

p. 55

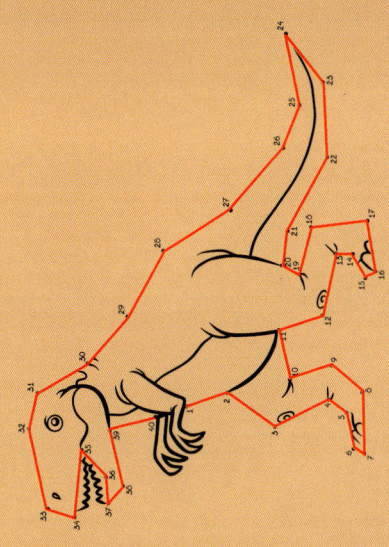
p. 56

p. 57

p. 58

Do you remember what Alberta word goes with the letter and the picture?

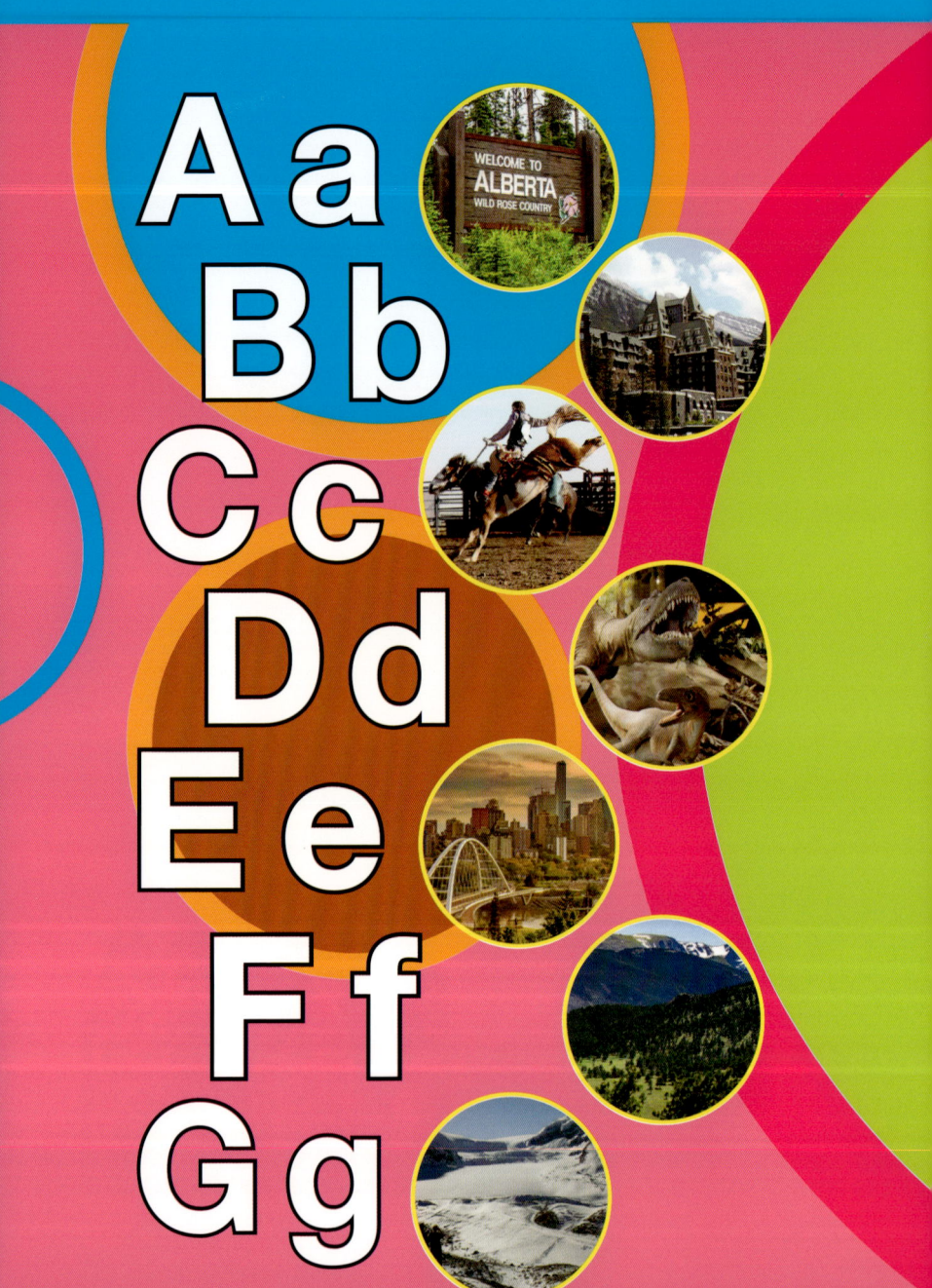

Hh Ii Jj Kk Ll Mm Nn

Do you remember what Alberta word goes with the letter and the picture?

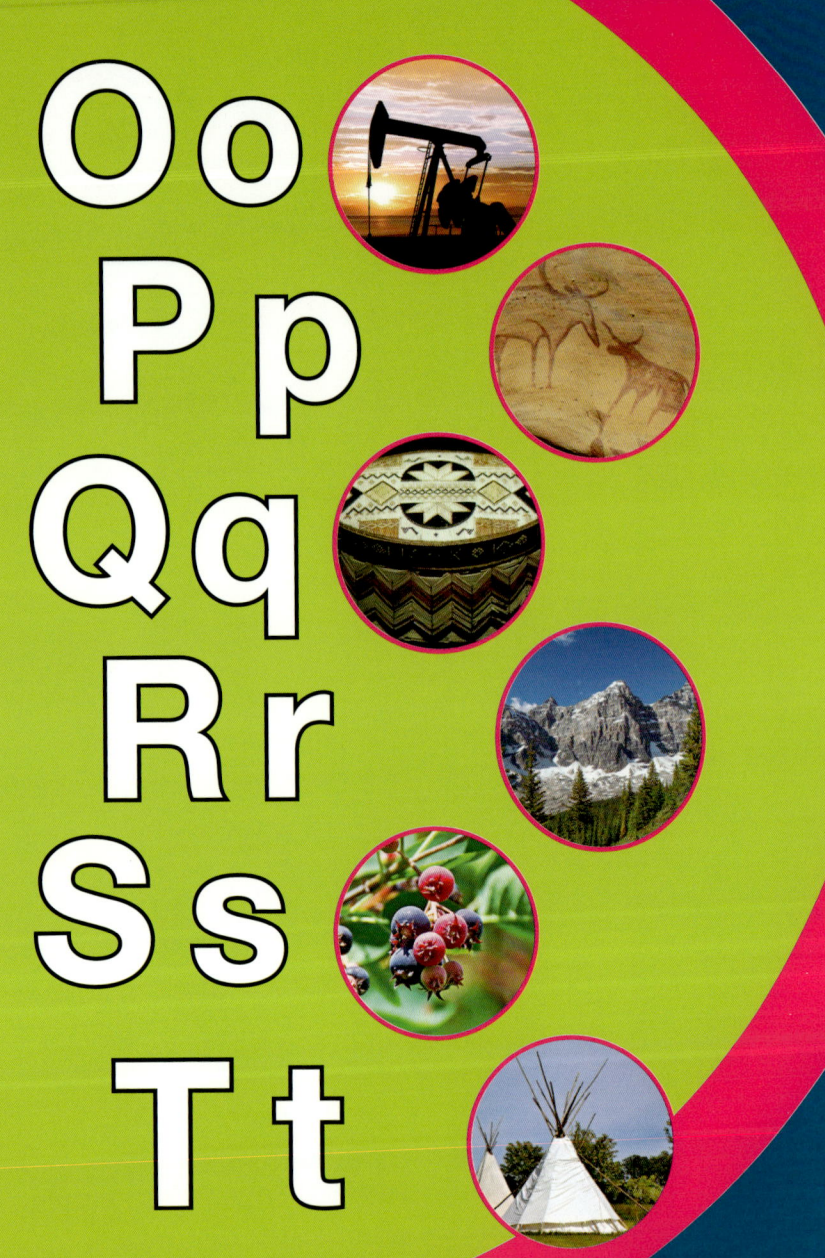